GOD'S GIFT

Eucharist

PRIMARY GRADES

for use in school and parish programs

LOYOLA**P**RESS.
A JESUIT MINISTRY

Nihil Obstat
Reverend Louis J. Cameli, S.T.D.
Censor Deputatus
December 10, 2007

Imprimatur
Reverend John F. Canary, S.T.L., D.Min.
Vicar General, Archdiocese of Chicago
December 11, 2007

Found to be in conformity
The Subcommittee on the Catechism, United States Conference of Catholic Bishops, has found this text, copyright 2009, to be in conformity with the *Catechism of the Catholic Church;* it may be used only as supplemental to other basal catechetical texts.

The *Nihil Obstat* and *Imprimatur* are official declarations that a book is free of doctrinal and moral error. No implication is contained therein that those who have granted the *Nihil Obstat* and *Imprimatur* agree with the content, opinions, or statements expressed. Nor do they assume any legal responsibility associated with publication.

Acknowledgments

Songs

"Children of the Lord" (page vi). Text and music by James V. Marchionda. Copyright © 1986, World Library Publications, Franklin Park, IL.
www.wlpmusic.com. All rights reserved. Used by permission.

"Your Word Is a Lamp" (page vi). Text and music by James V. Marchionda. Copyright © 2004, World Library Publications, Franklin Park, IL.
www.wlpmusic.com. All rights reserved. Used by permission.

"We Go Forth" (page vi). Text and music by James V. Marchionda. Copyright © 2004, World Library Publications, Franklin Park, IL. www.wlpmusic.com. All rights reserved. Used by permission.

Excerpts from the English translation of *The Roman Missal* © 2010, International Commission on English in the Liturgy Corporation. All rights reserved.

Loyola Press has made every effort to locate the copyright holders for the cited works used in this publication and to make full acknowledgment for their use. In the case of any omissions, the publisher will be pleased to make suitable acknowledgments in future editions.

Interior design: Kathy Greenholdt/Loyola Press, Think Design
Cover art: Susan Tolonen
Cover design: Think Design, Loyola Press
Art Director: Judine O'Shea/Loyola Press

For more information related to the English translation of the *Roman Missal, Third Edition,* see www.loyolapress.com/romanmissal.

ISBN-13: 978-0-8294-2666-3, ISBN-10: 0-8294-2666-3

Copyright © 2009 Loyola Press

LOYOLA PRESS.
A JESUIT MINISTRY

3441 N. Ashland Avenue
Chicago, Illinois 60657
(800) 621-1008
www.loyolapress.com

14 15 16 Web 10 9 8 7

Contents

As I open this book,
I remember how much God loves me
and calls me to be one with him
and all creation.

Thank you, God,
for giving me the Sacrament of the Eucharist
as a sign of your love and presence
in my life.

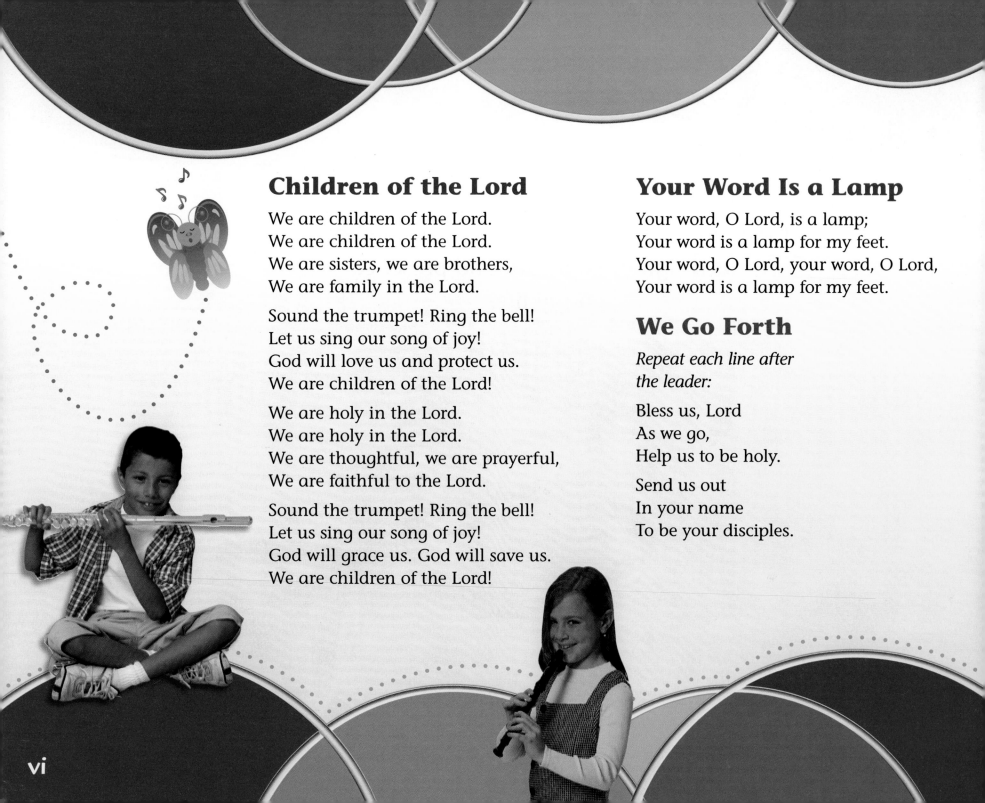

Children of the Lord

We are children of the Lord.
We are children of the Lord.
We are sisters, we are brothers,
We are family in the Lord.

Sound the trumpet! Ring the bell!
Let us sing our song of joy!
God will love us and protect us.
We are children of the Lord!

We are holy in the Lord.
We are holy in the Lord.
We are thoughtful, we are prayerful,
We are faithful to the Lord.

Sound the trumpet! Ring the bell!
Let us sing our song of joy!
God will grace us. God will save us.
We are children of the Lord!

Your Word Is a Lamp

Your word, O Lord, is a lamp;
Your word is a lamp for my feet.
Your word, O Lord, your word, O Lord,
Your word is a lamp for my feet.

We Go Forth

*Repeat each line after
the leader:*

Bless us, Lord
As we go,
Help us to be holy.

Send us out
In your name
To be your disciples.

Belonging

The Joy of Belonging

Belonging is good. It makes us feel safe. It makes us feel like a part of something bigger.

- I belong to a family. There are _____ people in my family.

- I belong to a parish. The name of our parish is _____.

- I belong in my neighborhood. I live on _____.

Loving God, help me to remember that I belong to you.

1

The Coming of the Holy Spirit

One day, Jesus' disciples and his mother, Mary, were praying together. All of a sudden, a mighty wind blew into the room with a roar. Flames like fire appeared over each person's head. Yet those in the room were not afraid. The Holy Spirit had come, just as Jesus had promised. Filled with the Holy Spirit, the disciples went out to tell the world about Jesus.

Many people heard the roar of the wind and gathered outside. The apostle Peter spoke to the crowd. He told them that Jesus died on the cross, rose from the dead, and ascended to heaven. He told them that from heaven, Jesus sent the Holy Spirit. He told the people that Jesus had come to save them.

adapted from Acts of the Apostles 2:1–4,32–41

Belonging to the Church

Many of the people who heard Peter preaching asked, "What do we have to do to be saved?" Peter told them to be sorry for their sins and to be baptized. The Acts of the Apostles tells us that about 3,000 people were baptized that day!

Like the people in the early Church, we are also baptized. At our **Baptism,** we are joined to Jesus and become members of the Catholic Church. We receive a permanent spiritual sign of God's grace. Baptism can never be repeated. We believe in the **Trinity:** God the Father, God the Son, and God the Holy Spirit. We believe that Jesus, the Son of God, became man to save us. Each time we make the Sign of the Cross, we remember our belief in the Trinity.

Unlike my sister, that baby doesn't cry at all!

My Baptism

Think about your own Baptism. What pictures
have you seen? What stories have you heard?
Draw a picture of your Baptism inside the
photo frame.

I Listen to God's Word

*Jesus told his disciples, "Baptize
them in the name of the Father,
and of the Son, and of the Holy
Spirit."*

adapted from Matthew 28:19

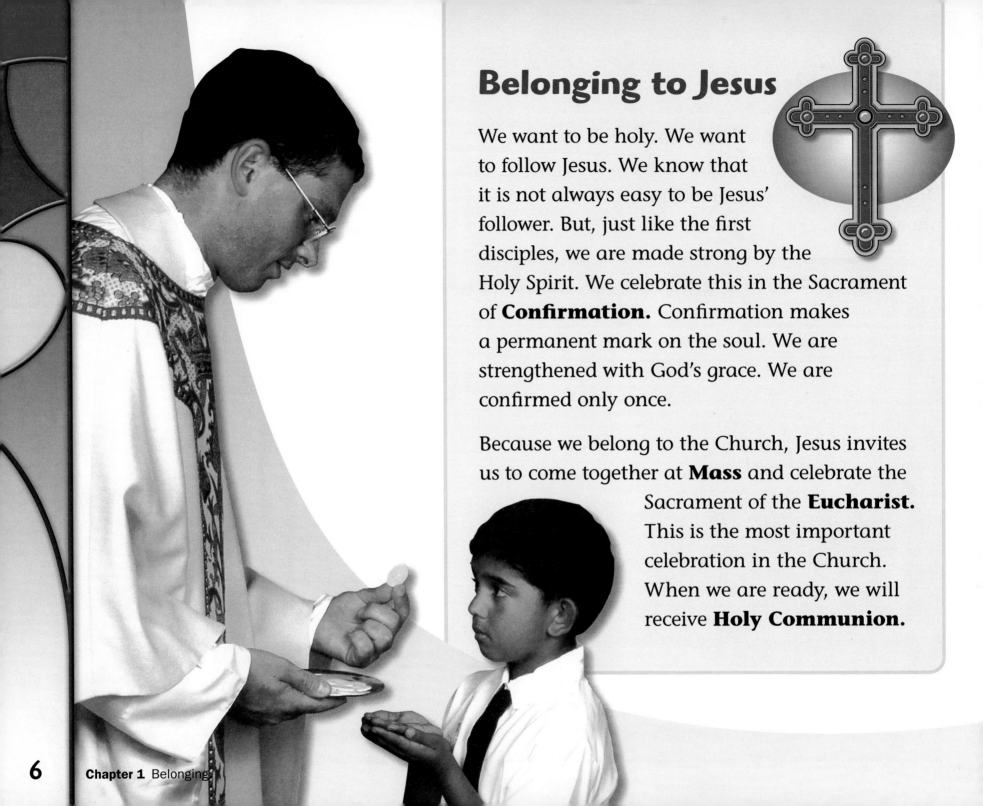

Belonging to Jesus

We want to be holy. We want to follow Jesus. We know that it is not always easy to be Jesus' follower. But, just like the first disciples, we are made strong by the Holy Spirit. We celebrate this in the Sacrament of **Confirmation.** Confirmation makes a permanent mark on the soul. We are strengthened with God's grace. We are confirmed only once.

Because we belong to the Church, Jesus invites us to come together at **Mass** and celebrate the Sacrament of the **Eucharist.** This is the most important celebration in the Church. When we are ready, we will receive **Holy Communion.**

What Am I?

Write the name of the object in the boxes next to it. The letters in the shaded boxes will tell you what helps you stay close to God.

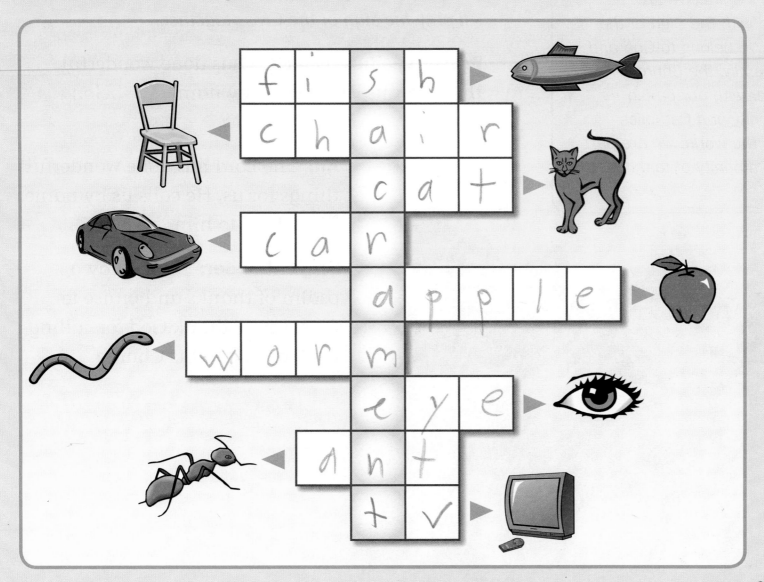

The Community of Faith

We are baptized in the name of the Trinity—Father, Son, and Holy Spirit. We are marked with the Sign of the Cross. We belong to God and to his family, the Church. Together with our parish community and Catholics around the world, we are part of a community of faith.

Baptized into Community

All pray the Sign of the Cross together.

Prayer Leader: The Lord has done wonderful things for us. He calls us by name. We belong to him.

All: The Lord has done wonderful things for us. He calls us by name. We belong to him.

Prayer Leader: Let us pray a psalm of thanks and praise to God. Let us thank God for calling us to belong to his Church.

Prayer Leader: Enter his gates with songs of praise. Give thanks to God and bless his name.

All: We are God's people; the sheep of his flock.

Prayer Leader: Give thanks to God and bless his name! His love lasts forever.

All: We are God's people; the sheep of his flock.

adapted from Psalm 100

Prayer Leader: We are all God's children. We are one with the Church all over the world. In praise and thanksgiving, we pray:

All: Glory be to the Father, and to the Son, and to the Holy Spirit. As it was in the beginning, is now, and ever shall be, world without end. Amen.

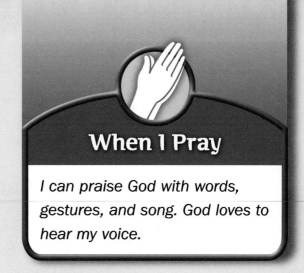

When I Pray

I can praise God with words, gestures, and song. God loves to hear my voice.

Living My Faith

I Remember What I Learn

- The disciples of Jesus received the Holy Spirit and baptized people.
- I am baptized. I belong to the Catholic Church.
- I believe in the Trinity: God the Father, God the Son, and God the Holy Spirit.
- I am invited to celebrate the Sacrament of the Eucharist.

I Live What I Learn

I prepare to receive the Body and Blood of Christ by

- living as a follower of Jesus.
- learning more about my faith.
- praying to the Holy Spirit.

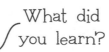

What did you learn?

I Share with My Family

How are baptisms celebrated in your family? Ask your parents and other relatives about their memories.

I Know These Words

Baptism	Holy Communion
Confirmation	Mass
Eucharist	Trinity

Closing Prayer

Thank you, God, for calling me to belong to your Church. Help me to grow in my faith.

Gathering

2

Family Times

It's fun to get together with grandparents, aunts, uncles, and cousins. Circle the special times when your whole family gathers.

Baptisms   holidays   picnics

birthdays   reunions   movie nights

weddings   vacations   Sunday dinners

At what other times does your family come together?

Loving God, help me to have a welcoming heart.

Welcoming the Ark of the Covenant

In the Old Testament of the Bible, we learn about the Ark of the Covenant. It was a large, brightly decorated, wooden box. There were wooden poles on each side of the Ark so people could carry it. On the top were two small angel sculptures. Inside the Ark were the stone tablets with the Ten Commandments.

The Ark of the Covenant was very special to the people of Israel. It was a sign of God's presence and love. The Ark traveled many miles with the people. King David had it carried to Jerusalem in a grand procession.

People gathered on the streets so they could see the Ark passing by. King David was especially happy. He was so happy that he sang and danced in front of the Ark. The people were also happy. They sang and played joyful music. The Ark reminded the people how much God loved them.

adapted from 2 Samuel 6:11–15

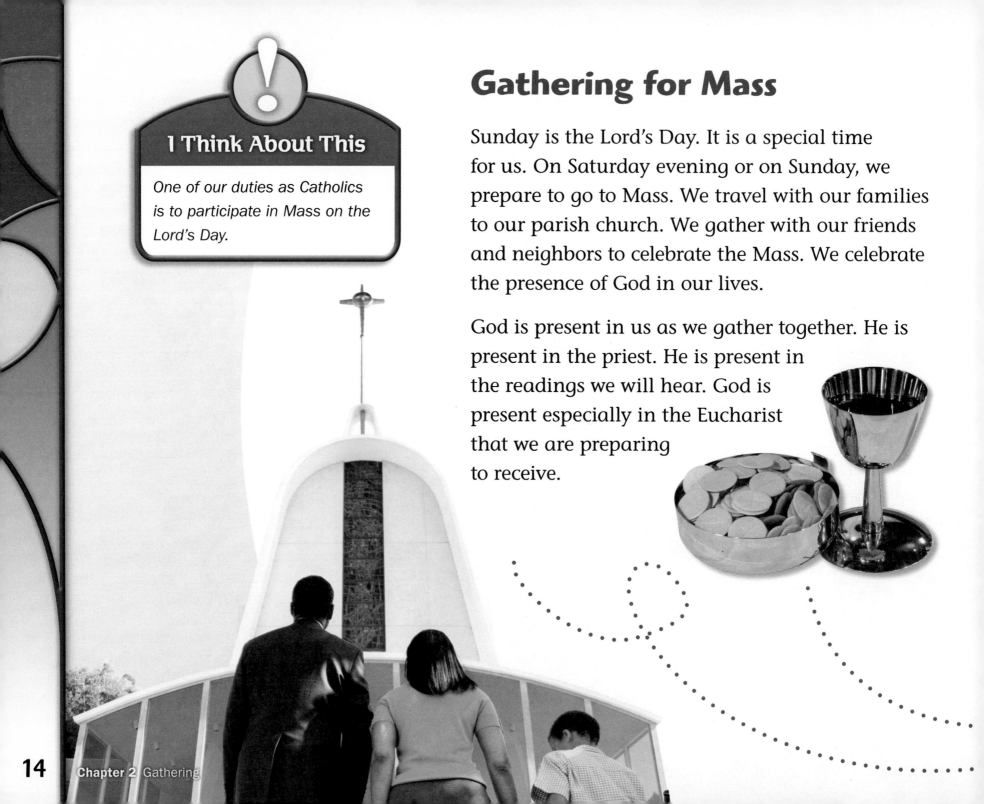

Gathering for Mass

Sunday is the Lord's Day. It is a special time for us. On Saturday evening or on Sunday, we prepare to go to Mass. We travel with our families to our parish church. We gather with our friends and neighbors to celebrate the Mass. We celebrate the presence of God in our lives.

God is present in us as we gather together. He is present in the priest. He is present in the readings we will hear. God is present especially in the Eucharist that we are preparing to receive.

Celebrating with My Family

Circle the right word. Fill in the blanks. Then color your home and your parish church.

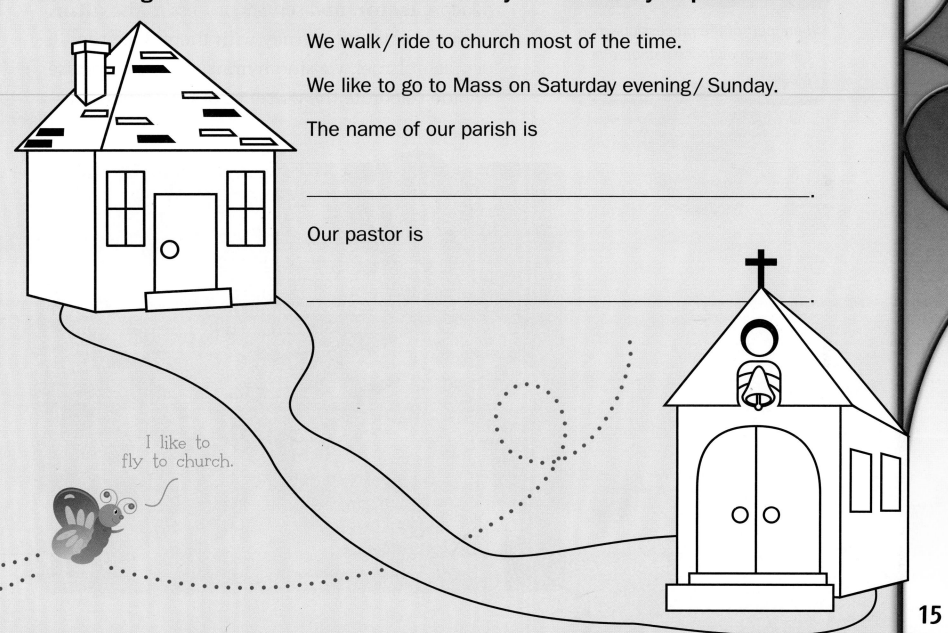

We walk / ride to church most of the time.

We like to go to Mass on Saturday evening / Sunday.

The name of our parish is

_____.

Our pastor is

_____.

I like to
fly to church.

When I Celebrate

I am part of the procession when I sing with all those gathered at Mass.

Celebrating God's Presence

We find a place to sit in church. Then the priest, deacon, **lector,** and servers process to the **altar.** In our hearts, we journey with them. Like the people of Israel, we sing hymns of joy and praise. We too celebrate the presence of God among us.

We begin Mass with the Sign of the Cross. The priest then greets us, saying:

The grace of our Lord Jesus Christ,
and the love of God,
and the communion of the Holy Spirit
be with you all.

We answer:

And with your spirit.

On the lines below, write your answer to the priest's welcome.

And with your spirit

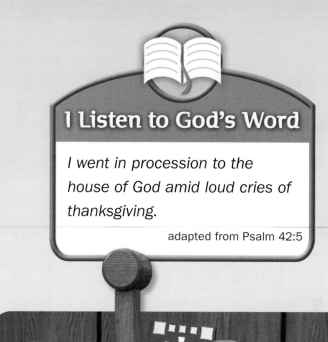

I Listen to God's Word

I went in procession to the house of God amid loud cries of thanksgiving.

adapted from Psalm 42:5

Filled with Joy

Knowing God's great love for us fills us with joy. Joy is a sign of God's presence. We recognize God in the people and things around us. We celebrate his presence with us when we go to Mass. We join with all those present to sing and pray with joy.

Singing and Dancing for God

Prayer Leader: God is with us! Let us rejoice and sing for joy!

All: Blessed be God forever!

Prayer Leader: In our own words, let's silently ask the Holy Spirit to help us hear God's Word.

Let's listen once more to the story of King David and the Ark.
(Welcoming the Ark of the Covenant, pages 12–13)

Now place yourself in the scene. Imagine that you are helping to carry the Ark of the Covenant. It is a special privilege. The Ark is a reminder of God's great love. There are many people walking with you. Some are praying; others are singing songs of praise and thanks to God. What would you like to praise God for today?

People line the road to watch the Ark pass by. Some have musical instruments. They play and sing and dance for joy as they think about God's great love for them. What joyful song do you know that you can sing to God?

All of a sudden, you notice that King David has come. He is so happy that he can't stand still. He begins to sing and dance too. All enter the city rejoicing.

Using your own words, silently thank God for his great love for you. Then pause for a moment and let God speak to you.

Praise be to God, who is always among us.

All: Blessed be God forever.

When I Pray

I remember how much God loves me. I can praise and thank him for all of the people and things that remind me of his love.

Living My Faith

I Remember What I Learn

- The Ark of the Covenant celebrates God's presence.
- I travel with my family to church.
- We gather to celebrate God's presence.
- We are welcomed by the priest.

I Live What I Learn

I go to Mass on the Lord's Day.

I celebrate God's presence.

I sing in praise of God.

I pray on the Lord's Day and all week too.

I Share with My Family

How do you enjoy the Lord's Day? Talk with your family about the ways you celebrate God's presence.

I Know These Words

altar

lector

Closing Prayer

Thank you, God, for your presence. I want to stay close to you.

Be sure to read pages 2–5 in your Mass booklet to learn more.

Reflecting

Sounds of Silence

Sit perfectly still.
Don't move at all—not your hands,
  nor your feet.
Breathe quietly.
Now close your eyes and listen.
Listen to the sounds around you.

What do you hear?

Ever-present God, help me to listen
for your voice in the world around me.

Standing on Holy Ground

The people of Israel lived in Egypt for a very long time. This was not a happy time for them. Day after day, they worked with little food and little rest. They were slaves, and they wanted to be free. They prayed to God for help. God chose Moses to help free them.

The Bible tells us about the day that God called Moses. Moses was busy taking care of his sheep on the mountainside. When he looked up, he noticed something strange. A bush was on fire, but it was not burning up.

Moses climbed the mountain to get a closer look. When he was near the bush, God spoke to him. God told him to take his sandals off. Moses did as he was told. He knew that he was standing on holy ground. He was in God's presence. God then sent Moses to rescue the people of Israel from Egypt.

adapted from Exodus 3:1–10

Knowing our Sinfulness

Moses got ready to meet God on his holy mountain. He took off his sandals. We get ready to celebrate the Mass. We turn our minds and hearts to God. We know that God will be present to us in a special way.

God wants to bring all of us together in love. But we know everything is not always all right with us. Sometimes we sin, and so we need to ask for God's forgiveness and **mercy.**

Sinning makes me so sad.

The priest or deacon leads us in a prayer of sorrow and forgiveness at Mass. We say:

Lord, have mercy.
Christ, have mercy.
Lord, have mercy.

This prayer reminds us that God's love and mercy are greater than our weakness.

When I Celebrate

Sometimes we say a prayer that begins "I confess to almighty God." After that prayer, we pray "Lord, have mercy."

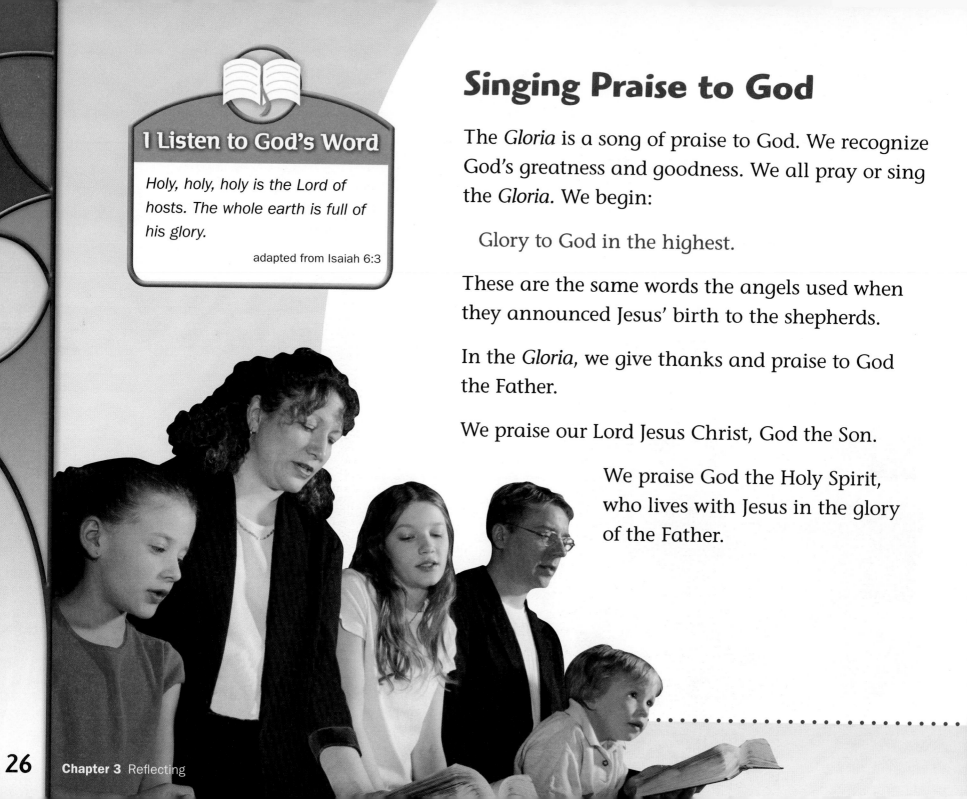

I Listen to God's Word

Holy, holy, holy is the Lord of hosts. The whole earth is full of his glory.

adapted from Isaiah 6:3

Singing Praise to God

The *Gloria* is a song of praise to God. We recognize God's greatness and goodness. We all pray or sing the *Gloria*. We begin:

Glory to God in the highest.

These are the same words the angels used when they announced Jesus' birth to the shepherds.

In the *Gloria*, we give thanks and praise to God the Father.

We praise our Lord Jesus Christ, God the Son.

We praise God the Holy Spirit, who lives with Jesus in the glory of the Father.

Living in Praise of God

Put a √ in the boxes that show children living in praise of God. On the lines, write something you will do this week to praise God.

_____

_____

Growing Still

When I remember that God loves me, I can open my heart to him. I tell God my joys and sorrows, my successes and failures. God's love is always there for me. When I let myself grow still, I can hear God's voice inside me and feel his presence.

Standing in God's Presence

Prayer Leader: As we make the Sign of the Cross together, we remember how much God loves us. In the name of the Father . . .

Response: Loving God, you call us, like Moses, to come close to you.

All: Glory to God in the highest!

Response: Loving God, your mercy is greater than our sinfulness.

All: Glory to God in the highest!

Response: Loving God, we join the angels in their song of praise.

All: Glory to God in the highest!

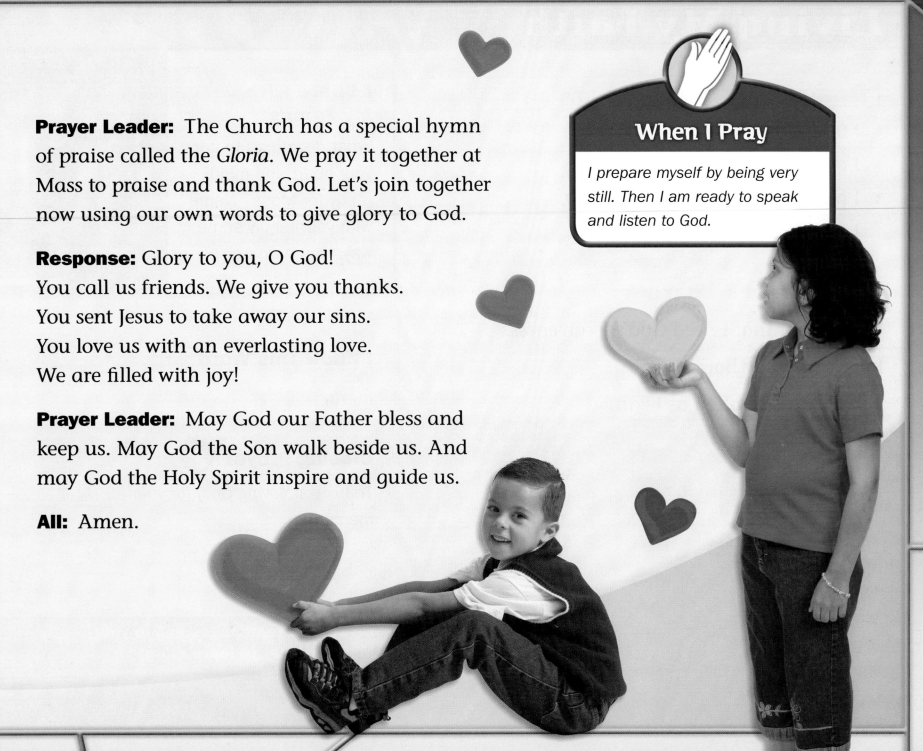

Prayer Leader: The Church has a special hymn of praise called the *Gloria*. We pray it together at Mass to praise and thank God. Let's join together now using our own words to give glory to God.

Response: Glory to you, O God!
You call us friends. We give you thanks.
You sent Jesus to take away our sins.
You love us with an everlasting love.
We are filled with joy!

Prayer Leader: May God our Father bless and keep us. May God the Son walk beside us. And may God the Holy Spirit inspire and guide us.

All: Amen.

When I Pray

I prepare myself by being very still. Then I am ready to speak and listen to God.

Living My Faith

I Remember What I Learn

- Moses got ready to meet God.
- I get ready for Mass.
- I pray for forgiveness and mercy.
- I sing "Glory to God."

I Live What I Learn

I remember that I need God's forgiveness.

I praise God by how I live.

I go to Mass as often as I can.

Isn't it wonderful that God forgives our sins?

I Share with My Family

What do you do to get your heart and mind ready for Mass? Name with your family some ways you prepare.

I Know This Word

mercy

Closing Prayer

Thank you, loving God, for your mercy.

Be sure to read pages 6–9 in your Mass booklet to learn more.

Listening

Story Time

Think of your favorite story.

What is it about?

Did someone read it to you?

Where were you when you first heard it or read it?

____ at home   ____ in school

____ at the library   ____ at a bookstore

____ at a family gathering

Jesus, Word of God, help me to listen to your stories with an open heart.

31

Planting and Growing

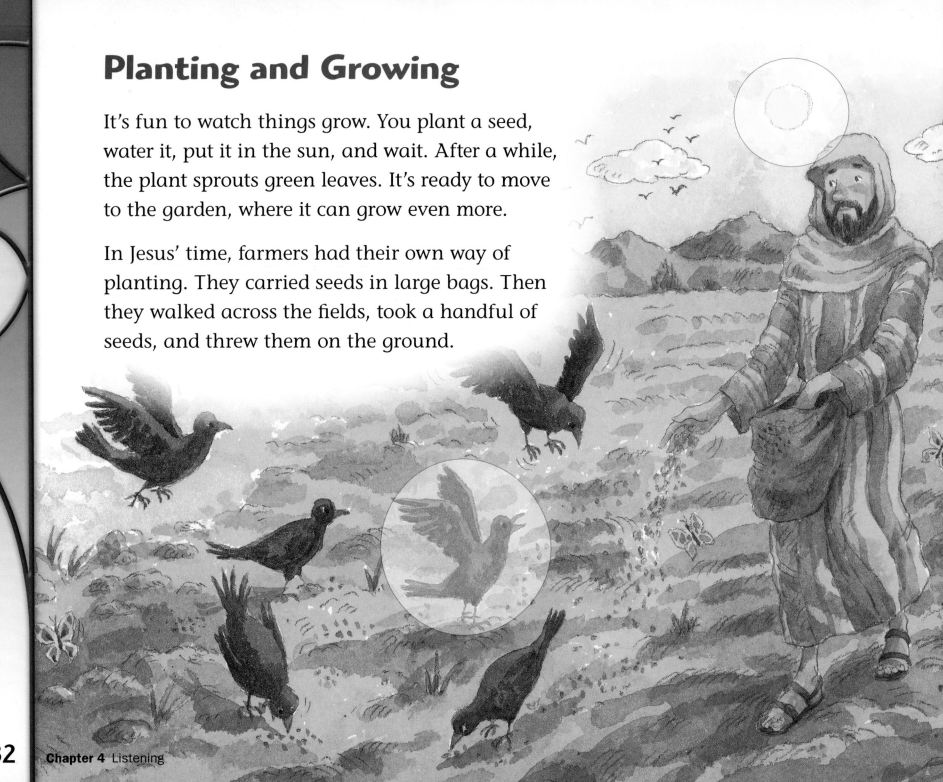

It's fun to watch things grow. You plant a seed, water it, put it in the sun, and wait. After a while, the plant sprouts green leaves. It's ready to move to the garden, where it can grow even more.

In Jesus' time, farmers had their own way of planting. They carried seeds in large bags. Then they walked across the fields, took a handful of seeds, and threw them on the ground.

Jesus tells the story of a farmer who did just that. Some of his seeds fell onto the road. The birds came and ate them up. Some fell among the rocks, where there was no place for the roots to grow. So when the sun came out, the plants dried up. Some seeds fell among thorns, which soon choked the young plants.

But some of the seeds fell on good ground. They grew deep roots. The plants became healthy and strong. The farmer was able to grow the food that he needed to live.

adapted from Matthew 13:3–8

Hearing God's Word

At Mass, we hear God's Word read from **Sacred Scripture.** God's Word is like the farmer's seeds. It is spoken for all to hear.

We sit during the First Reading, the Responsorial Psalm, and the Second Reading. Sitting means we are ready to listen and receive God's Word. Usually we hear a reading from the **Old Testament** or the Acts of the Apostles. Then we pray one of the **psalms.** Next is a reading from the **New Testament.** The lector reads from a special book called the *Lectionary for Mass.* After each reading, the lector says:

The word of the Lord.

We answer:

Thanks be to God.

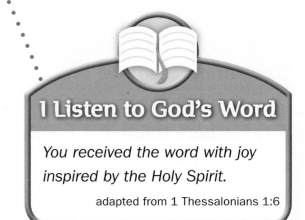

I Listen to God's Word

You received the word with joy inspired by the Holy Spirit.

adapted from 1 Thessalonians 1:6

We sing the Gospel Acclamation before the **Gospel** is read. Jesus is at the center of the Gospels. So we stand to hear these words. Standing gets us ready to hear something important. It helps us to pay attention to the words being spoken. In the Gospel Reading, Jesus speaks to us heart-to-heart. After the Gospel is read, the priest or deacon says:

The Gospel of the Lord.

We answer:

Praise to you, Lord Jesus Christ.

Next the priest or deacon gives the **Homily.** It helps us understand God's Word. It also helps us put into practice what we just heard.

Then we stand and pray the Profession of Faith or **Creed.** We state all that we believe. After the Creed, we ask God to hear our prayers for the world, the Church, our parish, and those in need.

Listening with Your Heart

We all hear God's Word at Mass. Some people hear, but they don't really pay attention to what they hear. God's Word becomes like the seed on the road. It dies.

Some people listen and think about what they heard. Then they forget about it. For them, God's Word is like a seed among the rocks or the thorns. It grows a little bit, and then it dies. God's Word has no chance to grow.

Remember what you know about a seed planted in good soil? You water it. You set it in the sun. You watch it grow. God's Word is like that. You listen, think about it, and remember God's Word. It can grow in you just like a seed in good ground.

Sharing God's Word

Think about the story of the farmer and the seed. In the boxes, draw pictures that tell the story. Be ready to talk about how the Word of God grows in your heart like the seed that grows in good soil.

Oh, how I

love

to draw!

1

2

3

4

We can be like good soil. When we listen carefully to God's Word, it grows in us, just like a seed in the ground. When we think about what we hear and what it means for us, the seed of God's Word grows strong. It helps us to live as faithful followers of Jesus.

You Are the Good Ground

All pray the Sign of the Cross together.

Prayer Leader: As we stand, ready to hear God's Word, let's pray silently that we will be the good ground where it will take root and grow.

Reader: A reading from the holy Gospel according to Matthew.

Jesus said, "A farmer went out to scatter seeds in a field. While the farmer was scattering the seeds, some fell along the road and were eaten by birds. Other seeds fell on rocky ground and quickly started growing because the soil was not very deep. But when the sun came out, the plants dried up. They did not have long enough roots. Other seeds fell where thorn bushes grew, and the thorns choked the plants. But some seeds fell on good ground. Their roots went deep into the earth. They grew strong and healthy."

adapted from Matthew 13:3–8

The Gospel of the Lord.

All: Praise to you, Lord Jesus Christ.

Prayer Leader: Let's sit comfortably, hands open in our laps, and think about what we just heard. Imagine yourself as the good soil. The story we just heard has been planted in your heart.

Talk with Jesus about the story and listen for what Jesus wants to say to you.

In gratitude, let us pray:

All: Jesus, Word of God, thank you for planting your seed in my heart. May your words be in my mind, on my lips, and in my heart. Help me to listen and understand and love you more each day. Amen.

When I Pray

I open myself to God's Word. It grows in me like a seed and helps me to live as a follower of Jesus.

Living My Faith

I Remember What I Learn

- God's Word is like seeds spread by the farmer.
- The homily helps me understand God's Word.
- God's Word grows in me when I listen and remember.

I Live What I Learn

I listen carefully to God's Word.

I pay attention to the homily.

I follow Jesus' teachings.

I'm listening as hard as I can!

I Share with My Family

Jesus often taught through stories. Ask your family members to share which Gospel story is their favorite.

I Know These Words

Creed	Old Testament
Gospel	psalm
homily	Sacred Scripture
New Testament	

Closing Prayer

Thank you, dear God, for planting your Word in my heart.

Be sure to read pages 10–16 in your Mass booklet to learn more.

Preparing

Company's Coming

We have much to do when someone special comes to visit. Toys need to be picked up. The house needs to be cleaned. Food needs to be prepared. All of this is done quickly and easily if everyone helps.

What is your special job when getting ready for company?

Loving Jesus, help me prepare my heart to receive you.

An Amazing Meal

A large crowd was listening to Jesus speak. They listened all day without anything to eat. Jesus knew they were hungry. He wanted to feed them. His disciples said that they had no food and that they had no money to buy food.

A young boy sitting near the disciples heard them talking. He offered to share the five small barley loaves and two fish he had brought for his lunch.

The apostle Andrew told Jesus about the boy's offer. But Andrew asked how two fish and a few loaves could feed so many.

Jesus took the boy's offering and gave thanks to God his Father. Then he told his disciples to share the food with all the people.

The disciples were amazed. Every time they reached into the basket, they found more food! Thousands of people were fed. The leftovers filled 12 large baskets.

The young boy gave what little he had. Jesus took his offering and multiplied it so that many could be fed. Then Jesus promised the people something even better. He promised to give himself as food.

adapted from John 6:1–13,47–51

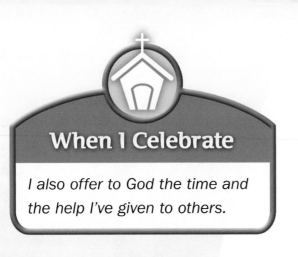

Presentation and Preparation of the Gifts

We bring the gifts of bread and wine to the altar. With the bread and wine, we give ourselves to God. Before this, there is a collection. It helps to support the work of the Church and to care for people in need.

The money we donate is also a gift of ourselves to God. All that we bring is joined with the gifts of bread and wine.

The Blessing of Our Gifts

The priest then prays prayers of **blessing.** He names the bread and wine as the gifts we bring. They are our way of saying thank you to God for his gifts to us. Finally, the priest praises God in prayer. He asks God to accept all that we bring.

We answer:

May the Lord accept the **sacrifice** at your
    hands
for the praise and glory of his name,
for our good
and the good of all his holy Church.

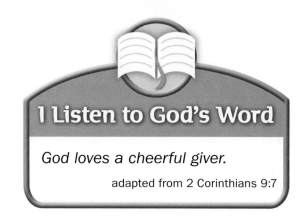

I Listen to God's Word

God loves a cheerful giver.

adapted from 2 Corinthians 9:7

I have a gift
for God too!

The size of my gift does not matter. What is important is the love that my gift shows.

An Even Greater Gift

Remember the young boy in the Gospel story? He had only a little bit to give. He offered it to Jesus. Jesus was able to take that little bit, those five barley loaves and two fish, and feed 5,000 people.

What we offer is important too. We offer the things we do for others as our gift to God. God takes the gifts we bring. In return, he gives us something much greater: the Body and Blood of Christ.

My Gift

Next to the gift box below, write things that you can do for others as your gift to God.

_____

_____

_____

_____

We All Have Gifts

Everyone has something to share. It might be our lunch, as it was for the boy in the Gospel story. It also can be a smile, a helping hand, or a kind word. God does wonderful things with whatever we have to give.

Gifts to Share

Prayer Leader: Blessed be God our Father who gave us Jesus, the greatest gift of all!

Response: Blessed be God forever!

Prayer Leader: When we share what we have with others, God's love turns our small gift into so much more. Let's bring all of our good deeds to God as we pray together:

Reader: We give you, O God, the good deeds we do for others.

Response: Receive our gift, we pray.

Reader: We give you, O God, the joy and laughter we bring into someone's day.

Response: Receive our gift, we pray.

Reader: We give you, O God, all of the times we remember to say thank you.

Response: Receive our gift, we pray.

Reader: We give you, O God, the kind words we speak.

Response: Receive our gift, we pray.

Prayer Leader: God calls us to share our gifts with others. This is one way we thank him for all that he has given us. We especially thank him for the gift of his Son, Jesus. In thanksgiving to God, let us pray together in the words that Jesus taught us.

All: Our Father, who art in heaven . . . Amen.

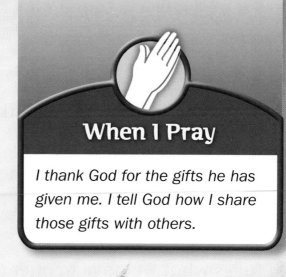

When I Pray

I thank God for the gifts he has given me. I tell God how I share those gifts with others.

Living My Faith

I Remember What I Learn

- The young boy offered to share the food that he brought.
- Jesus blessed the food and fed thousands.
- The priest blesses the bread and wine and my offering.
- God takes what we have to offer and increases it.

I Share with My Family

Each of us is blessed with special gifts. With your family, talk about how you each can use your gifts to live the way God wants.

I Live What I Learn

I have special gifts.

I can use my gifts and my time to help others.

I know that even small offerings are important.

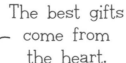

The best gifts come from the heart.

I Know These Words

blessing

sacrifice

Closing Prayer

Thank you, Jesus, for accepting what I offer. I will do my best to share my gifts.

Be sure to read pages 17–19 in your Mass booklet to learn more.

6

Remembering

The Best Gift Ever!

We all like to receive gifts. They are a sign that someone cares for us. Think about the gifts you've been given.

Do you have a favorite?

What is it?

Who gave it to you?

When was it given to you?

Do you still have it?

Jesus, gift of God, help me to remember that you are the greatest gift of all.

Jesus Keeps His Promise

Remember the Gospel story about the boy with the five loaves and two fish? After feeding the hungry crowd, Jesus promised the people something even better. He promised he would give himself as food.

Jesus gave us this food at the **Last Supper.** On the night before he died on the cross, Jesus shared one last meal with his apostles.

During supper, he took bread, blessed it, broke it, and gave it to his disciples, saying: "This is my body, which will be given for you; do this in memory of me."

Jesus then took the cup of wine, blessed it, and gave it to his disciples, saying: "This chalice is the new covenant in my blood, which will be shed for you."

adapted from Luke 22:14–20

The food that Jesus gave us is his own Body and Blood under the form of bread and wine. This is the food we need as we journey to heaven.

Jesus suffered and died on the cross. We celebrate his sacrifice at Mass.

A Prayer of Thanksgiving

The **Eucharistic Prayer** is the high point of our celebration of the Mass. It is our prayer of praise and thanksgiving. In it, we remember all that Jesus has done to save us. We remember Jesus' sacrifice on the cross. He gave up his life to save us from sin. We receive the grace of salvation that Jesus won for us.

The priest begins this prayer.

All then join with him in singing or saying:

Holy, Holy, Holy Lord God of hosts.
Heaven and earth are full of your glory.
Hosanna in the highest.
Blessed is he who comes in the name of the Lord.
Hosanna in the highest.

The dove is a symbol of the Holy Spirit.

The Real Presence

The next part of the Eucharistic Prayer is the **consecration.** At this time, through the words and action of the priest, Jesus' sacrifice is made present again. The priest repeats the very same words Jesus said at the Last Supper. The bread and wine then become the Body and Blood of Christ.

The Body and Blood of Christ will look and taste like bread and wine. They have become the Body and Blood of Christ through the power of the Holy Spirit and the priest's words of consecration.

Our Spiritual Food

Next, all sing or pray:

> We proclaim your Death, O Lord,
> and profess your Resurrection
> until you come again.

In the Eucharistic Prayer, we offer
the bread and wine as a sign of offering
ourselves to God. In return, God gives us the
Eucharist, the Body and Blood of Jesus Christ.
Under the appearance of bread and wine, Christ
himself becomes our spiritual food. We will
receive him when we receive Holy Communion.
Realizing all of this, we sing or pray together:

> Amen.

This Amen is our yes to all that has taken place.
It brings the Eucharistic Prayer to an end.

Words to Remember

Find and circle these words.

Last Supper   Amen   thanksgiving

Holy Communion   consecration   offering

```
F  U  S  T  C  A  Y  H  L  I  O  H  U  Z
G  H  A  I  O  G  W  H  A  M  F  X  H  T
A  D  M  A  N  P  X  F  S  I  F  Y  O  E
C  A  U  A  S  L  E  H  T  U  E  G  B  H
F  P  S  H  E  I  U  H  S  I  R  A  H  P
H  O  L  Y  C  O  M  M  U  N  I  O  N  T
A  T  C  A  R  I  S  H  P  I  N  H  D  I
B  X  Y  D  A  M  E  N  P  T  G  U  F  G
F  P  P  H  T  M  S  H  E  I  W  H  U  H
C  H  A  I  I  I  S  H  R  I  U  D  H  A
P  Z  E  H  O  U  T  S  G  Y  P  P  E  Z
C  T  H  A  N  K  S  G  I  V  I  N  G  H
```

One with Jesus

At Mass, we remember how much Jesus loves us. We remember how he shared a meal with his apostles. We remember how he gave himself to them as a gift. Jesus is with us in a special way. When we receive him in Holy Communion, we are one with him and with one another.

The Love That Makes Us One

Prayer Leader: As we pray the Sign of the Cross, we remember that God's great love for us makes us all brothers and sisters.

All pray the Sign of the Cross together.

Prayer Leader: To prepare ourselves to hear the Word of God, let's silently ask the Holy Spirit to help us be good listeners.

Now listen once more to the story of the Last Supper.

(Jesus Keeps His Promise, pages 52–53)

Imagine that you are at the table with Jesus and the apostles. The table is filled with plates of special food. In the center of the table is a roasted lamb. There are baskets of bread and glasses of wine. Everything smells delicious. Look around the table. What else do you notice?

You see Jesus take a piece of bread from the basket. Everyone grows silent when he starts to pray a blessing. He looks at each of you and says "This is my body, which will be given for you; do this in memory of me." What do you think about when you hear those words?

It is hard to understand Jesus' words. But it is easy to understand Jesus' love for you. You understand that you are united with him in love. Jesus gives us the gift of himself because he loves us all so much.

Thank Jesus for the great love he has for you. Then pause for a moment and let him speak to you.

All: I give thanks to you, O LORD.
I thank you with all my heart.
For you have given good things
To all those who love you. Amen.

adapted from Psalm 138:1–2

When I Pray

I remember how much I am loved by Jesus. I thank him for the gift of himself in the Eucharist.

Living My Faith

I Remember What I Learn

- Jesus gave us his Body and Blood at the Last Supper.
- The priest prays the words of consecration.
- Jesus Christ is present in Holy Communion through the action of the Holy Spirit.
- Holy Communion is food for my spiritual journey.

I Live What I Learn

I listen carefully to the words of consecration at Mass.

I believe that Jesus Christ is really present in the Eucharist.

I prepare myself for my first Holy Communion.

Oh my! You really learned a lot in this chapter!

I Share with My Family

Christ is present to us in Holy Communion. Talk with your family about the times you feel God's presence in your home too.

I Know These Words

consecration

Eucharistic Prayer

Last Supper

Closing Prayer

Thank you, loving Jesus, for the gift of your Body and Blood. Help me to have a great love for the Eucharist.

Be sure to read pages 20–23 in your Mass booklet to learn more.

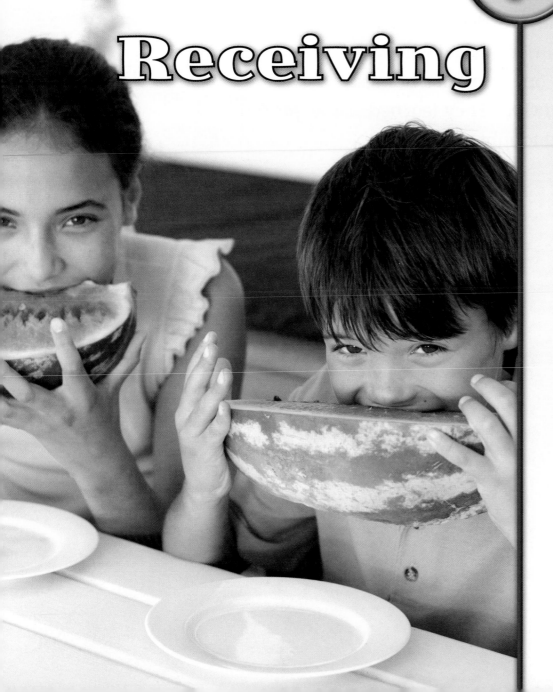

7

Receiving

Good for You

We all want to be healthy. That means we eat foods that make us strong and give us energy. Circle the foods below that are healthy choices.

carrots	jelly beans	chicken
potato chips	milk	soda pop
oatmeal	apples	wheat bread
cheese	ice pops	cupcakes

Jesus, Bread of Life, strengthen me to do your will.

The Early Christians

At the Last Supper, Jesus told the apostles, "Do this in memory of me." The early Christians did what Jesus wanted. They gathered in one another's homes. They sang hymns. They praised God. They learned more about what Jesus said and taught.

The people also remembered what Jesus did on the night of the Last Supper. They remembered what Jesus told them to do. They blessed and broke the bread. They blessed the chalice of wine. They received the Body and Blood of Christ.

adapted from Acts of the Apostles 2:42–47

Communion Rite

We get ready to receive Holy Communion at Mass. We pray as Jesus taught us. We pray the Lord's Prayer.

Fill in the missing words so that you can pray with the priest and the people at Mass.

Our Father, who art in heaven,

hallowed be thy _____;

thy kingdom come,

thy _____ be done

on earth as it is in heaven.

Give us this day our daily _____,

and forgive us our trespasses,

as we _____ those who trespass
    against us;

and lead us not into temptation,

but _____ us from evil.

Amen.

The priest continues to pray. He asks God again to protect us from evil and to give us peace. He prays that we will be free from sin and full of hope.

Then together we say:

> For the kingdom,
> the power and the glory are yours
> now and for ever.

The Sign of Peace follows the Lord's Prayer. At this time, we share a sign of peace with one another and pray for God's mercy.

I Think About This

The Lord's Prayer is also called the Our Father. It is the prayer that Jesus taught us.

Receiving Holy Communion

We sing as we come in procession to receive Holy Communion. Before we receive the **host,** we bow our heads. The priest, the deacon, or the extraordinary minister of Holy Communion says:

The Body of Christ.

We answer:

Amen.

This is our yes. It means we really believe that we are receiving Jesus Christ. The priest then places the host in our hand or on our tongue.

When we receive the Blood of Christ, we again bow our heads and answer:

Amen.

Then we drink from the **chalice.**

Praying After Communion

After we receive Holy Communion, we return to our place in church. Jesus has come to us. He is our spiritual food. He gives us the grace and strength we need to be his followers. He helps us to avoid sin in the future. We welcome him into our hearts. Then, after everyone has received Communion, we pray in silence.

Think about what you will want to say to Jesus after you receive your first Holy Communion. Write your prayer here.

_____

_____

_____

_____

I Listen to God's Word

Thanks be to God for his great gift!

adapted from 2 Corinthians 9:15

I wonder what she's saying to Jesus.

*Jesus taught his apostles
to pray the Lord's Prayer.
We know that prayer too.
When we pray it together,
we remember that God is
our Father. We are all his
children. God wants us to
have all that we need.*

All That We Need

Prayer Leader: When his apostles asked Jesus how to pray, he taught them the Our Father. As we pray it slowly together, let's think about what it means for us today.

All: Our Father, who art in heaven, hallowed be thy name;

Prayer Leader: God is our Father. He made us. He loves us. His name is holy. We speak it reverently, with respect.

All: thy kingdom come,
thy will be done
on earth as it is in heaven.

Prayer Leader: We grow in holiness when we care for God's creation. We show that we care for nature, for ourselves, and for other people.

All: Give us this day our daily bread,

Prayer Leader: God is generous. All that we have is a gift from him. He wants us to have everything we need.

All: and forgive us our trespasses, as we forgive those who trespass against us;

Prayer Leader: God wants us to forgive others, just as he forgives us.

All: and lead us not into temptation, but deliver us from evil. Amen.

Prayer Leader: God is our Father. He gives us the grace to follow Jesus. We thank him as we pray together:

All: We praise and thank you, loving God, through Jesus Christ, your Son. Amen.

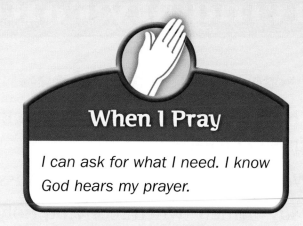

When I Pray

I can ask for what I need. I know God hears my prayer.

Living My Faith

I Remember What I Learn

- The first Christians received the Body and Blood of Christ.
- We pray the Lord's Prayer at Mass.
- I say "Amen" when receiving Holy Communion.

I Live What I Learn

I learn the words of the Our Father.

I believe that Christ is truly present in the consecrated bread and wine.

I thank Jesus for inviting me to receive him in Holy Communion.

Don't worry. I'll be very quiet while you pray.

I Share with My Family

Jesus shares himself with us in the Eucharist. With your family, name ways each of you shares your time and love with others.

I Know These Words

chalice

host

Closing Prayer

Thank you, Jesus, for teaching me to pray.
Help me to open my heart to you.

Be sure to read pages 24–30 in your Mass booklet to learn more.

Journeying

8

On the Way

Part of the fun of going away is getting ready. Imagine you're going on vacation or to camp. You'll be away for a while. What three things will you be sure to pack in your suitcase?

1. _____

2. _____

3. _____

Jesus, faithful friend, help me to walk with you so that I can spread your Word to others and live in your love.

The Man on the Road

Two of Jesus' followers were on a journey. They were leaving Jerusalem. Jesus, their friend, had died on the cross there.

Along the way, the two friends met a man on the road. He asked them why they were so sad. They told him that their friend Jesus had died. Some women had said that Jesus had risen from the dead, but they were not sure what to believe.

The man began to walk with the two friends. He reminded them that the Scriptures said that God would send a savior who would suffer, die, and then enter heaven.

As evening came, the three travelers arrived at a village. The two friends invited the man to stay for dinner with them. At dinner, the man took bread, blessed it, broke it, and gave it to them.

At that moment, the friends knew that this man was the risen Jesus! Then Jesus disappeared.

The friends went happily back to Jerusalem. They told everyone there that they had seen the risen Jesus.

adapted from Luke 24:13–35

Our Journey

We are like Jesus' friends on their journey from Jerusalem. They welcomed Jesus. They knew him in the breaking of the bread. Then they went back to Jerusalem. They wanted to tell everyone that Jesus is still with us.

We too are on a journey—our journey of faith. We recognize Jesus in the Eucharist. We welcome Jesus into our hearts. We welcome him in the people we meet. We share his love with others. We want everyone to know about Jesus and all that he does for us.

I'm going to spread the Word with you.

Final Blessing

After we have received Holy Communion, we take time to sit or kneel quietly. It is a time to thank Jesus.

Then, the priest stands for the Final Blessing. We stand too. Sometimes the priest or deacon tells us to bow our heads and pray for God's blessing. He asks God for a number of special graces for us.

Then we bless ourselves as the priest prays:

May almighty God bless you,
the Father, and the Son, and the Holy Spirit.

We answer:

Amen.

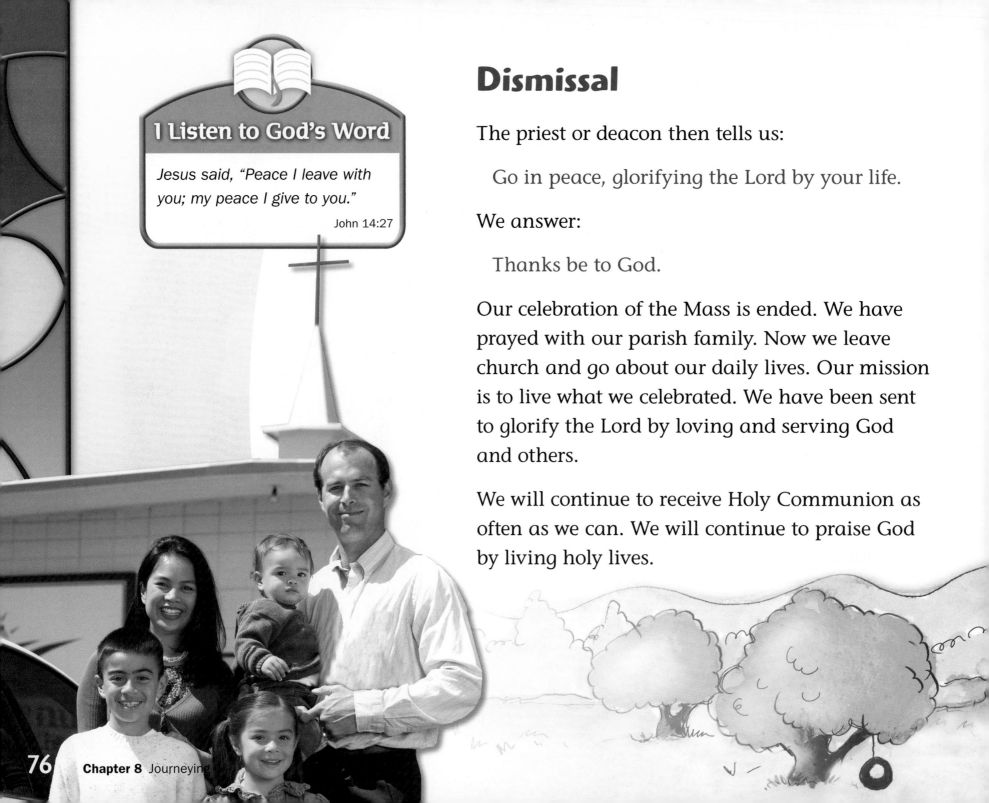

Jesus said, "Peace I leave with you; my peace I give to you."

John 14:27

Dismissal

The priest or deacon then tells us:

Go in peace, glorifying the Lord by your life.

We answer:

Thanks be to God.

Our celebration of the Mass is ended. We have prayed with our parish family. Now we leave church and go about our daily lives. Our mission is to live what we celebrated. We have been sent to glorify the Lord by loving and serving God and others.

We will continue to receive Holy Communion as often as we can. We will continue to praise God by living holy lives.

Loving and Serving Others

In each of the buildings, write or draw something you can do to glorify the Lord by bringing the love of Jesus to others.

Home

Church

School

Sent to Share

Receiving Jesus Christ in Holy Communion is a wonderful gift. It's a gift that is meant to be shared. Jesus gives himself to us so that we can share his love with others.

Blessed and Sent

Pray the Sign of the Cross together.

Prayer Leader: Just like the two friends who met Jesus on the road, we meet Jesus. We talk with him and open our hearts to him. Soon you will share in the holy meal of the Sacrament of the Eucharist. Let us open our hearts to Jesus, who sends us to love and serve others.

Lord Jesus, you bless me with your presence in my life.

Response: Send me with your joy to glorify the Lord.

Prayer Leader: Lord Jesus, you bless me with your Word in the Gospels.

Response: Send me with your peace to glorify the Lord.

Prayer Leader: Lord Jesus, you bless me with the desire to receive you in Holy Communion.

Response: Send me with your love to glorify the Lord.

Prayer Leader: Lord Jesus, you bless me with the gift of being your friend.

Response: Send me with your grace to glorify the Lord.

Prayer Leader: God our Father, you love us. Keep us always in your care.

Response: Amen.

Prayer Leader: Jesus, you are our friend and brother. Fill our hearts with unending love.

Response: Amen.

Prayer Leader: Holy Spirit, you strengthen us. Help us to live a life of love and service.

Response: Amen.

Prayer Leader: Go in peace, glorifying the Lord by your life.

Response: Thanks be to God.

Pray the Sign of the Cross together.

When I Pray

I ask for God's blessing for myself and for others.

Living My Faith

I Remember What I Learn

- The friends of Jesus knew him in the breaking of the bread.
- I will meet Jesus in Holy Communion.
- I am sent to bring Jesus' love to others.

I Live What I Learn

I love Jesus.

I follow Jesus.

I will receive Jesus Christ in Holy Communion.

I will bring his peace and love to others.

Friend, always go in peace.

I Share with My Family

After Mass, we are sent to bring Christ's love to others. Discuss with your family what you will remember and bring from your preparation for Holy Communion.

Closing Prayer

Thank you, Jesus, for this special time of preparation. Help me to always look forward to receiving you with joy.

Be sure to read pages 31–32 in your Mass booklet to learn more.

I Live My Faith

I Celebrate the Lord's Day

Sunday is the day on which we celebrate the Resurrection of Jesus. Sunday is the Lord's Day. We begin our celebration of the Lord's Day on Saturday evening. To celebrate the Lord's Day, we gather for Mass. We rest from work. We spend time with our families and do things for others. People all over the world gather at God's Eucharistic Table as brothers and sisters.

The Order of Mass

Mass is the high point of our faith life as Catholics. It always follows a set order.

Introductory Rites

We gather as a community to celebrate God's presence in our lives. We praise God singing together the **Entrance Chant.**

We all pray the **Sign of the Cross.** Then the priest greets us in the words of the **Greeting:**

Priest: The grace of our Lord Jesus Christ, and the love of God, and the communion of the Holy Spirit be with you all.

People: And with your spirit.

Penitential Act

We acknowledge our sinfulness and ask God for mercy. The priest may invite us to pray this prayer:

I confess to almighty God
and to you, my brothers and sisters,
that I have greatly sinned,
in my thoughts and in my words,
in what I have done and in what I have
   failed to do,

Then, we strike our breast and say:

through my fault, through my fault,
through my most grievous fault;
therefore I ask blessed Mary ever-Virgin,
all the Angels and Saints,
and you, my brothers and sisters,
to pray for me to the Lord our God.

Kyrie

Then we pray for God's mercy and forgiveness:

Priest: Lord, have mercy.
People: Lord, have mercy.

Priest: Christ, have mercy.
People: Christ, have mercy.

Priest: Lord, have mercy.
People: Lord, have mercy.

Priest: May almighty God
   have mercy on us,
forgive us our sins,
and bring us to
   everlasting life.
People: Amen.

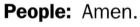

Gloria

Together we praise God in prayer by singing or saying the *Gloria.*

Glory to God in the highest,
and on earth peace to people of good will.

We praise you,
we bless you,
we adore you,
we glorify you,
we give you thanks for your great glory,
Lord God, heavenly King,
O God, almighty Father.

Lord Jesus Christ, Only Begotten Son,
Lord God, Lamb of God, Son of the
   Father,
you take away the sins of the world,
   have mercy on us;
you take away the sins of the world,
   receive our prayer;
you are seated at the right hand of the
   Father,
   have mercy on us.

For you alone are the Holy One,
you alone are the Lord,
you alone are the Most High,
Jesus Christ,
with the Holy Spirit,
in the glory of God the Father.
Amen.

Collect Prayer

We ask God to hear our prayers.
First, we all pray in
silence. Then the
priest prays aloud,
and we respond
"Amen."

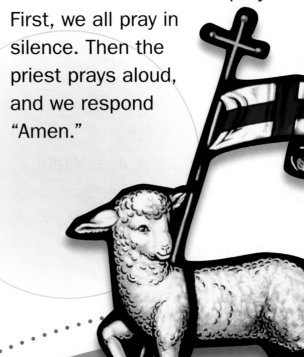

Liturgy of the Word

We listen to God's Word proclaimed from Sacred Scripture. We sit during the first two readings. We stand as the Gospel is proclaimed. We listen to the homily and pray that God's Word will take root in our hearts.

First Reading

We listen to God's Word, usually from the Old Testament or the Acts of the Apostles. We honor God's Word by our response.

Lector: The word of the Lord.
People: Thanks be to God.

Responsorial Psalm

We respond to God's Word in the Psalm. The lector or cantor invites us to pray the words of the Psalm, usually in song.

Second Reading

We listen to God's Word from the books of the New Testament: one of the Letters or the Book of Revelation. We thank God for speaking his Word to us.

Lector: The word of the Lord.
People: Thanks be to God.

Gospel Reading

We stand and, except during Lent, we sing "Alleluia!" to praise God for the Good News we will hear in the Gospel. We prepare to listen to a reading from one of the Gospels.

Priest or deacon: The Lord be with you.
People: And with your spirit.

Priest or deacon: A reading from the holy Gospel according to . . .
People: Glory to you, O Lord.

Then all trace a cross on their foreheads, lips, and hearts. We pray that God's Word will be in our minds, on our lips, and in our hearts.

The priest or deacon proclaims the Gospel. We offer praise for the Good News we hear in the Gospel.

Priest or deacon: The Gospel of the Lord.
People: Praise to you, Lord Jesus Christ.

Homily

We sit and listen as the priest or deacon explains God's Word. He helps us understand how to live out what we have heard.

Profession of Faith

I believe in one God,
the Father almighty,
maker of heaven and earth,
of all things visible and invisible.

I believe in one Lord Jesus Christ,
the Only Begotten Son of God,
born of the Father before all ages.
God from God, Light from Light,
true God from true God,
begotten, not made, consubstantial with
  the Father;
through him all things were made.
For us men and for our salvation
he came down from heaven,
and by the Holy Spirit was incarnate of
  the Virgin Mary,
and became man.

For our sake he was crucified under
  Pontius Pilate,
he suffered death and was buried,
and rose again on the third day
in accordance with the Scriptures.
He ascended into heaven
and is seated at the right hand of the Father.
He will come again in glory
to judge the living and the dead
and his kingdom will have no end.

I believe in the Holy Spirit, the Lord, the
  giver of life,
who proceeds from the Father and the Son,
who with the Father and the Son is adored
  and glorified,
who has spoken through the prophets.

I believe in one, holy, catholic and apostolic
  Church.
I confess one Baptism for the forgiveness of
  sins
and I look forward to the resurrection of the
  dead
and the life of the world to come. Amen.

Prayer of the Faithful
We ask God to hear our prayers for the
Church, for the world, for people
in need, and for ourselves.

Liturgy of the Eucharist

The bread and the wine become the Body and Blood of Christ. We receive this most precious gift in Holy Communion.

Presentation and Preparation of the Gifts

Gifts of bread and wine are brought to the altar. The priest then prepares the altar.

The priest lifts up the bread and prays a prayer, sometimes aloud. We respond "Blessed be God for ever."

Then he raises the wine and says a prayer, sometimes aloud. We respond the same way.

We stand as the priest prays over the gifts. He asks God to accept our sacrifice.

Priest: Pray, brothers and sisters, that my sacrifice and yours may be acceptable to God, the almighty Father.

People: May the Lord accept the sacrifice at your hands for the praise and glory of his name, for our good and the good of all his holy Church.

Eucharistic Prayer

This prayer of thanksgiving is the center and high point of the entire celebration.

In the **Preface,** the priest invites us to stand and give thanks to God.

Priest: The Lord be with you.
People: And with your spirit.

Priest: Lift up your hearts.
People: We lift them up to the Lord.

Priest: Let us give thanks to the Lord our God.
People: It is right and just.

The priest continues praying words of thanks and praise. Then we all pray in praise of God as we sing or say the ***Holy, Holy, Holy:***

Holy, Holy, Holy Lord God of hosts.
Heaven and earth are full of your glory.
Hosanna in the highest.
Blessed is he who comes in the name of
  the Lord.
Hosanna in the highest.

We kneel during the **Consecration.** The priest prays the words that Jesus spoke at the Last Supper. Through the power of the Holy Spirit and the words and actions of the priest, the bread and wine become the Body and Blood of Jesus Christ.

The Mystery of Faith

We remember all that Jesus has done to save us.

The priest or deacon invites us to proclaim the mystery of our faith.

We sing or say aloud this prayer or another:

We proclaim your Death, O Lord, and profess your Resurrection until you come again.

The priest continues to pray the words of the Eucharistic Prayer, asking God to receive our sacrifice of praise. He joins our prayer with the prayers of the whole Church. We pray quietly as we listen to the words of the Eucharistic Prayer.

Then the priest prays the **Concluding Doxology.** We respond Amen. When we pray **Amen,** we are saying yes in faith to all that we have prayed in the Eucharistic Prayer.

Priest: Through him, and with him, and in him,
O God, almighty Father,
in the unity of the Holy Spirit,
all glory and honor is yours,
for ever and ever.

People: Amen.

Communion Rite

Now we prepare to receive the Body and Blood of Jesus Christ. We pray to be united with one another in Christ.

We stand and pray together
The Lord's Prayer:

Our Father, who art in heaven,
hallowed be thy name;
thy kingdom come,
thy will be done
on earth as it is in heaven.
Give us this day our daily bread,
and forgive us our trespasses,
as we forgive those who trespass
  against us;
and lead us not into temptation,
but deliver us from evil.

Sign of Peace

The priest prays that we will be united with one another in Christ's peace.

Priest: The peace of the Lord be with you always.
People: And with your spirit.

Then the priest or deacon invites us to offer a sign of peace to those around us. We exchange a greeting of peace such as "The peace of the Lord be with you always."

The priest breaks the consecrated host. We all sing or say aloud the **Lamb of God:**

Lamb of God, you take away the sins of
  the world,
have mercy on us.
Lamb of God, you take away the sins of
  the world,
have mercy on us.
Lamb of God, you take away the sins of
  the world,
grant us peace.

Communion

We kneel. The priest raises the Body of Christ and the chalice with the Blood of Christ and prays:

Priest: Behold the Lamb of God,
behold him who takes away the sins of
   the world.
Blessed are those called to the supper
   of the Lamb.

We respond:

People: Lord, I am not worthy
that you should enter under my roof,
but only say the word
and my soul shall be healed.

The priest receives Holy Communion. Then he offers the Body and Blood of Christ to the deacon and to the extraordinary ministers of Holy Communion.

We receive the Body of Christ—under the form of bread—in our hands or on our tongue. We bow our heads.

Priest: The Body of Christ.
People: Amen.

We receive the Blood of Christ under the form of wine. We bow our heads.

Priest: The Blood of Christ.
People: Amen.

After we receive Holy Communion, we return to our place to pray quietly in our own words. We thank Jesus for the gift of himself in the Eucharist.

After a time of silent prayer, the priest invites us to stand and leads the **Prayer after Communion.** We ask God to help us live as Jesus has called us to live.

Concluding Rites

We continue standing as the priest invites us to pray.

Priest: The Lord be with you.

People: And with your spirit.

The priest offers the **Final Blessing.** We make the Sign of the Cross.

Priest: May almighty God bless you, the Father, and the Son, and the Holy Spirit.

People: Amen.

In the **Dismissal,** we are sent to glorify the Lord by loving and serving him and one another, to continue the mission given to us at Mass.

Priest or deacon: Go in peace, glorifying the Lord by your life.

People: Thanks be to God.

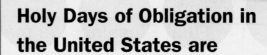

I Remember These Things About Holy Communion

I Respect These Rules for Receiving Holy Communion

I fast for one hour before receiving Holy Communion. I do not have any food or drink, except water or medicine.

I am in the state of grace, free from mortal sin.

I receive Holy Communion as often as possible.

I participate at Mass on Sundays and on Holy Days of Obligation.

I receive Holy Communion at least once each year during the Easter season.

> **Holy Days of Obligation in the United States are**
>
> - January 1—Mary, the Mother of God
>
> - 40 days after Easter or the Seventh Sunday of Easter— Ascension of the Lord
>
> - August 15—Assumption of the Blessed Virgin Mary
>
> - November 1—All Saints
>
> - December 8—Immaculate Conception of the Blessed Virgin Mary
>
> - December 25—Nativity of the Lord

I Receive Holy Communion with Reverence

When the Body and Blood of Christ are offered to me, I bow.

To receive Holy Communion in my hands, I extend my hands with my palms facing up, dominant hand below the other hand.

The priest or the extraordinary minister of Holy Communion says "The Body of Christ."

I reply "Amen."

After receiving the Body of Christ, I pick it up with my dominant hand and place it in my mouth.

If I choose to receive Holy Communion on my tongue, then after I say "Amen," I fold my hands, open my mouth, and extend my tongue. After the Body of Christ has been placed on my tongue, I close my mouth.

The priest or extraordinary minister of Holy Communion offers the chalice and says "The Blood of Christ."

I reply "Amen."

I then take the chalice in my own hands. I sip a small amount of the Blood of Christ and then return the chalice.

After receiving Holy Communion, I return to my place in church and pray.

I Pray These Prayers

Sign of the Cross

In the name of the Father,
and of the Son,
and of the Holy Spirit. Amen.

The Lord's Prayer

Our Father, who art in heaven,
hallowed be thy name;
thy kingdom come,
thy will be done
on earth as it is in heaven.
Give us this day our daily bread,
and forgive us our trespasses,
as we forgive those who trespass
  against us;
and lead us not into temptation,
but deliver us from evil.
Amen.

Glory Be to the Father

Glory be to the Father,
and to the Son,
and to the Holy Spirit.
As it was in the beginning,
is now, and ever shall be,
world without end. Amen.

Hail Mary

Hail Mary, full of grace,
the Lord is with you.
Blessed are you among women,
and blessed is the fruit of your
  womb, Jesus.
Holy Mary, Mother of God,
pray for us sinners,
now and at the hour
  of our death.
Amen.

Apostles' Creed

I believe in God,
the Father almighty,
Creator of heaven and earth,
and in Jesus Christ, his only Son, our Lord,
who was conceived by the Holy Spirit,
born of the Virgin Mary,
suffered under Pontius Pilate,
was crucified, died and was buried;
he descended into hell;
on the third day he rose again from the dead;
he ascended into heaven,
and is seated at the right hand of God the
   Father almighty;
from there he will come to judge the living
   and the dead.

I believe in the Holy Spirit,
the holy catholic Church,
the communion of saints,
the forgiveness of sins,
the resurrection of the body,
and life everlasting. Amen.

Prayer Before Meals

Bless us, O Lord, and these your gifts
which we are about to receive from
   your goodness.
Through Christ our Lord.
Amen.

Prayer After Meals

We give you thanks
for all your gifts,
almighty God,
living and reigning
now and for ever.
Amen.

Morning Prayer

God, our Father,
I offer you today
all that I think and do and say.
I offer it with what was done
   on earth
by Jesus Christ, your Son.
Amen.

Here is a sticker activity for you.
Your catechist will guide you.

I Know These Words

altar

altar the table in the church on which the priest celebrates Mass. On the *altar*, the bread and wine are offered to God to become the Body and Blood of Jesus Christ.

Baptism the sacrament that frees us from original sin and gives us new life in Jesus Christ through the Holy Spirit. *Baptism* is the first of the three Sacraments of Initiation by which we become full members of the Church. The other two Sacraments of Initiation are Confirmation and the Eucharist.

Bible the written story of God's promise to care for us, especially through his Son, Jesus. We listen to readings from the *Bible* at Mass.

blessing a prayer that calls for God's power and care upon some person, place, thing, or activity. At the end of Mass, the priest gives us a *blessing* and tells us to go in peace.

chalice

chalice the cup used for the consecration of wine at Mass. I drink from the *chalice* when I receive the Blood of Christ in Holy Communion.

Confirmation the sacrament that completes the grace we receive in Baptism. *Confirmation* is the Sacrament of Initiation in which we are made stronger in our faith. The other two Sacraments of Initiation are Baptism and the Eucharist.

consecration the bread and wine become the Body and Blood of Christ by the power of the Holy Spirit and the words and actions of the priest. The *consecration* is part of the Eucharistic Prayer.

creed a summary of what people believe. The Apostles' *Creed* is a summary of Christian beliefs.

Eucharist the sacrament in which the Body and Blood of Christ is made present under the form of bread and wine. The *Eucharist* is the Sacrament of Initiation in which we give praise and thanks to God for giving us Jesus Christ. The other two Sacraments of Initiation are Baptism and Confirmation.

Eucharistic Prayer the central part of the Mass when the sacrifice of Jesus is made present again through the words and actions of the priest. At Mass, the *Eucharistic Prayer* is our prayer of thanksgiving.

Gospels

Gospel the Good News of God's love for us. In the *Gospels* of Matthew, Mark, Luke, and John, we learn the story of Jesus' life, Death, Resurrection, and Ascension.

grace the gift of God given to us without our earning it. *Grace* fills us with God's life and makes us his friends.

Holy Communion the consecrated bread and wine that we receive at Mass. In *Holy Communion,* we receive the Body and Blood of Christ.

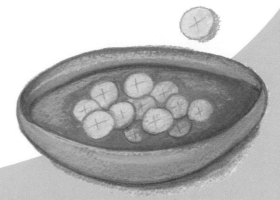

Holy Communion

hosts

Homily an explanation of God's Word. The *Homily* explains how to live according to the message we hear in the readings at Mass.

host the unleavened bread used at Mass. Consecrated *hosts* are kept in the tabernacle.

Last Supper the last meal Jesus ate with his disciples on the night before he died. Every Mass is a remembrance of the *Last Supper.*

lector the person who proclaims the Word of God at Mass. At Mass, we listen to the *lector* read from the Old and New Testaments.

Mass our most important way of praying to God. At *Mass,* we listen to God's Word and receive Jesus Christ in Holy Communion.

mercy kindness and forgiveness offered to another. When we sin, we ask for God's *mercy.*

mercy

New Testament the second part of the Bible. In the *New Testament,* we read the story of Jesus and the early Church.

Old Testament the first part of the Bible. In the *Old Testament,* we read the story of how God prepared the people for the coming of Jesus.

psalm a prayer in the form of a poem. There are 150 *psalms* in the Old Testament Book of Psalms.

sacrament one of seven ways through which God's life enters our lives by the power of the Holy Spirit. The seven *sacraments* are Baptism, Confirmation, Eucharist, Reconciliation, Anointing of the Sick, Holy Orders, and Matrimony.

Sacraments of Initiation the three sacraments that make us full members of the Church. The *Sacraments of Initiation* are Baptism, which frees us from original sin; Confirmation, which strengthens our faith; and the Eucharist, in which we receive the Body and Blood of Christ.

Sacred Scripture the holy writings of Jews and Christians collected in the Old and New Testaments of the Bible. At Mass, we hear God's Word proclaimed from *Sacred Scripture.*

sacrifice a gift given to God to give him thanks. Jesus' death on the cross was the greatest *sacrifice.*

Trinity the mystery of one God existing in three Persons. God the Father, God the Son, and God the Holy Spirit are the *Trinity.*

Trinity

Index

Scripture Index

Art Credits

All butterfly art by Kathryn Seckman Kirsch

Front Matter
iii(b) Jupiter Images
vi(l) Phil Martin Photography

Chapter 1
1 Edgardo Contreras/Getty Images
2–3 Anna Leplar
5(l) iStockphoto.com/Michael Tupy
6(l) Myrleen Ferguson Cate/Photo Edit
6(r) iStockphoto.com/Alejandro Raymond
8(l) *Baptism,* the Aguilar family. The Girard Foundation Collection. The Museum of International Folk Art, Santa Fe, New Mexico. Photo by Michael Monteaux.
9(l) Guillermina Aguilar
9(r) Guillermina Aguilar
10 Phil Martin Photography

Chapter 2
12–13 Anna Leplar
14(r) W. P. Wittman Limited
15 Mia Basile
16(l) Jupiter Images
16(r) Tony Freeman/Photo Edit
17 Phil Martin Photography

Chapter 3
21 Steven Puetzer/Getty Images
22–23 Anna Leplar
25(r) Phil Martin Photography
29(r) Phil Martin Photography
30 Phil Martin Photography

Chapter 4
32–33 Anna Leplar
35 Myrleen Ferguson Cate/Photo Edit
36–37(hearts) iStockphoto.com/Loon Yik Herng
39 Joy Allen

Chapter 5
42–43 Anna Leplar
44(arm) Jupiter Images
44(basket) iStockphoto.com/Aldra
44(priest/family) Myrleen Ferguson Cate/Photo Edit
46(hands) iStockphoto.com/Pathathai Chungyam
46–47 Joy Allen
48(l) Jose Luis Pelaez Inc./Getty Images
49(illustrations) iStockphoto.com/Achim Prill

Chapter 6
52–53 Anna Leplar
56(l) Kathryn Seckman Kirsch
57(r) iStockphoto.com/John Woodcock

Chapter 7
62–63 Anna Leplar
64(t) P. Deliss/Godong/CORBIS
65(l) iStockphoto.com/H. Tuller
65(r) The Crosiers/Gene Plaisted OSC
66(br) iStockphoto.com/Jim Jurica
68–69 Joy Allen

Chapter 8
72–73 Anna Leplar
75(l) iStockphoto.com/Alejandro Raymond
75(r) Myrleen Ferguson Cate/Photo Edit
77 Joy Allen
78(tl) Jupiter Images

I Live My Faith
83 Phil Martin Photography
84 The Crosiers/Gene Plaisted OSC
85(b) Phil Martin Photography
86 Alamy/ArkReligion.com
88(l) Phil Martin Photography
90 Myrleen Ferguson Cate/Photo Edit
91(t) Phil Martin Photography
93(t) Phil Martin Photography
93(b) Michael Newman/Photo Edit
94(t) iStockphoto.com/Julie de Leseleuc
94(b) Jupiter Images
95 Myrleen Ferguson Cate/Photo Edit
96 The Crosiers/Gene Plaisted OSC
98–99 Phyllis Pollema-Cahill

I Know These Words
100–103 Susan Tolonen

Chapter 4 / Capítulo 4

Chapter 3 / Capítulo 3

apter 6 / Capítulo 6

Chapter 5 / Capítulo 5

Estas son las calcomanías para usar en la página 98 de tu libro. Tu catequista te indicará el momento para usarlas.

lector	cáliz
pila bautismal	hostias
Evangelario	diácono
monaguillos	sacerdote
ambón	ministro extraordinario de la Sagrada Comunión
cruz procesional	
crucifijo	sagrario
altar	cantor

© LOYOLAPRESS. God's Gift: Eucharist.

estas personas y cosas durante la misa

Here are your stickers for pages 98–99 of your book. Your catechist will let you know how to use them.

lector	chalice
baptismal font	hosts
Book of the Gospels	deacon
altar servers	priest
ambo	extraordinary minister of Holy Communion
processional cross	
crucifix	tabernacle
altar	leader of song

© LOYOLAPRESS. God's Gift: Eucharist.

I See These People and Things at Mass